Do squirrels swarm?

No! Locusts swarm.

A locust is a type of grasshopper. Thousands of locusts form a dark, dangerous cloud. They swarm through the sky and attack crops. Hungry locusts can strip a cornfield bare.

4

Do squirrels hunt in packs?

No! Wolves hunt in packs.

Wolves hunt for food in groups called packs. Either the strongest female wolf or the strongest male leads the pack. Together, a pack of wolves can attack and bring down larger animals, such as moose or elk.

Animals All Around

Do Squirrels Swarm?

A Book About Animal Groups

by Michael Dahl
illustrated by Franklin Ayers

Special thanks to our advisers for their expertise:

Kathleen E. Hunt, Ph.D.
Research Scientist & Lecturer, Zoology Department
University of Washington, Seattle, Washington

Susan Kesselring, M.A., Literacy Educator
Rosemount-Apple Valley-Eagan (Minnesota) School District

PICTURE WINDOW BOOKS
MINNEAPOLIS, MINNESOTA

Managing Editor: Bob Temple
Creative Director: Terri Foley
Editor: Peggy Henrikson
Editorial Adviser: Andrea Cascardi
Copy Editor: Laurie Kahn
Designer: Todd Ouren
Page production: BANTA Digital Group
The illustrations in this book were rendered digitally.

Picture Window Books
5115 Excelsior Boulevard
Suite 232
Minneapolis, MN 55416
1-877-845-8392
www.picturewindowbooks.com

Printed in the United States of America.

Library of Congress Cataloging-in-Publication Data
Dahl, Michael.
Do squirrels swarm? : a book about animal groups / by Michael Dahl ; illustrated
by Franklin Ayers.
p. cm. — (Animals all around)
Summary: Introduces a number of different animals and the names of the groups
in which they live, travel, or work.
Includes bibliographical references (p.   ).
ISBN 1-4048-0287-8 (lib. bdg.)
1. Animal behavior—Juvenile literature. [1. Animal behavior.]
I. Ayers, Franklin, 1962—, ill. II. Title.
QL751.5 .D33 2004
591.5—dc22
2003016530

Do squirrels swim in schools?

No! Dogfish sharks swim in schools.

Dogfish sharks travel in schools of hundreds or thousands.
Sometimes, the males swim in one school and the females swim
in another. The huge schools follow cool currents through the ocean.

Do squirrels migrate?

No! Monarchs migrate.

Every autumn, millions of monarch butterflies migrate to escape the cold winter. Huge clouds of monarchs fly from Canada and the northern United States to southern California and Mexico.

Do squirrels stampede?

No! Zebras stampede.

Zebras gallop as a group to flee from enemies such as lions.
Zebras stampede so fast that their stripes seem to blur together.
An attacking lioness gets confused. She can't tell one zebra
from another!

Do squirrels flock?

No! Flamingos flock.

Flamingos fly, feed, sleep, and nest together in groups called flocks. They rely on the many eyes of the flock to watch for danger.

Do squirrels graze in herds?

No! Cattle graze in herds.

Herds of cows and bulls with broad shoulders roam through green pastures. They graze on grass and tender plants. A hungry herd might chew a field nearly bare before moving on to new grazing grounds.

16

Do squirrels huddle?

No! Penguins huddle.

Emperor penguins huddle in the freezing winds. They keep each other warm with their fat, feathery bodies. The penguins take turns standing on the cold outer edge of the cozy crowd.

Do squirrels live in colonies?

No! Ants live in colonies.

Ants live in giant families called colonies. Each colony has a queen, who is the mother of all the other ants. Most of her daughters are the worker ants that gather food. Some are new queens. The sons and new queens are flying ants. They zoom off to start new colonies.

Do squirrels scamper alone?

Yes! Squirrels scamper alone.

Not all animals gather in large groups. Squirrels scamper alone along tree branches, hunting for nuts and acorns. Some kinds of squirrels won't even allow other squirrels into their territories.

How Animals Live—Together or Alone

Animals search for food together.

wolves	hunt in packs
cattle	graze in herds

Animals stay safe together.

zebras	stampede
flamingos	flock

Animals stay warm together.

monarchs	migrate
penguins	huddle

Some animal groups have many members.

locusts	swarm in fields
dogfish sharks	swim in schools
ants	live in colonies

Some animals live by themselves.

squirrels	scamper alone

Glossary

colony—a group whose members live and work together. Ants live in a colony.

flock—to gather in a group. This word usually refers to birds. Some kinds of birds flock to find food and keep each other safe.

herd—a large group of animals, such as cows or horses, that move together as they feed

huddle—to crowd tightly together in a group. Some animals huddle for safety or warmth.

migrate—to move from one area to another. Some birds and monarch butterflies migrate south to find warmer weather before winter comes.

pack—a group of animals, such as wolves, that live and hunt together

scamper—to run or move lightly and quickly

school—a group of underwater creatures that swim together

swarm—to gather or fly close together in a large group. Locusts and bees swarm.

Index

To Learn More

At the Library

Hovanec, Erin M. *I Wonder What It's Like to Be an Ant.* New York: PowerKids Press, 2000.

Olien, Rebecca. *Squirrels: Furry Scurriers.* Mankato, Minn.: Bridgestone Books, 2002.

Raatma, Lucia. *Penguins.* Minneapolis: Compass Point Books, 2001.

Schaefer, Lola M. *Wolves: Life in the Pack.* Mankato, Minn.: Bridgestone Books, 2001.

Senack, J. Elaine. *Memories of a Monarch.* Torrington, Conn.: House Finch Press, 2001.

On the Web

Fact Hound offers a safe, fun way to find Web sites related to this book. All of the sites on Fact Hound have been researched by our staff.
http://www.facthound.com

1. Visit the Fact Hound home page.
2. Enter a search word related to this book, or type in this special code: 1404802878.
3. Click on the FETCH IT button.

Your trusty Fact Hound will fetch the best sites for you!